The Co-Planner:
Two Professionals + One Plan for Co-Teaching

Fourth Edition

Lisa A. Dieker, Ph.D.
University of Central Florida

KNOWLEDGE
by Design, Inc.

Whitefish Bay, Wisconsin

The Co-Planner: Two Professionals + One Plan for Co-Teaching (4th ed.).

ISBN: 978-1-941171-00-4

Printed in the United States of America.

Ordering Information

See the order form on last page of this book or visit our web site:
http://www.knowledge-by-design.com

About the Author

Lisa Dieker is the Pegasus Professor and Lockheed Martin Eminent Scholar Chair at the University of Central Florida. She coordinates the doctoral program in special education and is Director of the Lockheed Martin Mathematics and Science Academy. Her primary area of research focuses on collaboration between general and special education. She has a passion for how technology can impact teacher preparation and student learning. She has received more than $15 million in grant funding and published over 50 chapters and journal articles. She coordinates several field-based grants and has had the opportunity to observe schools and classrooms throughout the United States and internationally.

Author Contact Information:

Lisa Dieker, Ph.D.
Professor and Lockheed Martin Eminent Scholar Chair
Department of Child, Family and Community Sciences
College of Education - 315M
University of Central Florida
P.O. Box 161250
Orlando, FL 32816-1250
email: lisa.dieker@ucf.edu

Acknowledgements

I would like to thank the numerous teachers, administrators and colleagues who have shared ideas and granted me access to their classrooms to develop this book. The ideas presented have all been observed in actual practice.

I want to specifically thank the following people who have contributed to both my knowledge base and the material in this book. I would like to acknowledge that the following pages have been developed or modified from material presented by my colleagues:
  pp. 6-7 lesson plans were created by Dianne Kelley and Gail Wranovsky
  Week 28 testing ideas were modified from material created by Janet Hill
  Research and development of the reflective frameworks were modified from my work with Lisa Monda-Amaya.

This book is dedicated to all professionals who value and commit to collaboration to ensure the success of all students.

How to Use this Co-Planner

Lisa A. Dieker, Ph.D.

Purpose

The use of co-teaching is on the rise at all levels of education. Research has demonstrated that co-teaching is an effective instructional strategy, when implemented correctly, for enhancing the success of students with disabilities in general education classrooms (see pp. 10-11 for a research reading list). However, as many teachers have discovered, new tools are needed to support the collaborative planning and communication required to make co-teaching successful.

Current lesson plan structures do not address the needs of both co-teachers. Nor do plan books allow space for planning and documenting individual accommodations for students with disabilities. This book was designed to facilitate collaborative planning between two educators and provide documentation of accommodations and modifications made for students with disabilities.

Unique Features

Teachers will appreciate many unique features found in this plan book:
- Creates shared planning by educators completing the weekly plan.
- Offers side-by-side view of planning and meeting state standards.
- Allows educators to document the interventions used, and progress made toward IEP or RTI goals.
- Supports educators as they evaluate, refine, and continue their development as co-teachers.
- Provides notes from the author for insight into the value, art, and the impact of co-teaching.

Features for Educators

Like most lesson plan books, space is provided to outline lesson activities and assessment procedures for each class subject and period. The lead educator uses the left page to record the "big ideas" and goals of each co-taught lesson. This format is easy to implement and requires no additional planning time beyond the time spent with a traditional plan book.

Educators complete the modified assessments column on the left-hand page of the book for any academic or behavioral needs of a student as well as the right-hand page.

The co-teachers will also note the types of co-teaching models the team will use, academic and behavioral adaptations needed for specific students, materials that may be needed to meet all students' needs as well as a place to jot notes to each other or about student performance related to IEP goals and objectives. Using this format ensures that what is special about special education is maintained throughout the co-taught setting.

The plan book also has two new areas of emphases. The all/some objective box reminds two teachers to ensure that they are planning their objective for what they want ALL students to do/know (everyone can name the stages of Mitosis), but also with two teachers to support differentiation it is important to also be prepared to challenge students who are advanced in a concept. Hence when the objectives are written one teacher might focus on the minimum level of mastery (ALL) and one might think about how to enrich or enhance the baseline skill for advanced learners, which has to be part of the planning process.

Outcomes and Benefits

Given concern for the success of all students, space is offered for both teachers to identify students who need additional accommodations or who are at-risk of failing in the class (see top box on each page). Interventions planned by the educator may be used to assist all students.

As with any plan book, this model only works if both co-teachers are committed to preparing lessons in advance so that they can effectively meet the needs of all students. As a result of using *The Co-Planner*, you will notice the following benefits:
- Clarified roles of both teachers,
- Combined ownership of planning,
- Improved instructional planning for meeting the needs of individual students,
- Increased collaboration in lesson development and delivery,
- Improved documentation of the development and use of specific accommodations for reporting IEP progress.

Remember that communication and evaluation are the keys to successful co-teaching relationships. I hope this new structure helps you be more effective as you work together to ensure the success of all students.

Dr. Dieker Describes the New Features

As my work in co-teaching has evolved and the field has advanced concerning inclusionary educational practices, a few additional features have been included in the 4th edition of the co-planner.

I have included examples of lessons plans not only across the various types of co-teaching but also an example of an elementary versus a secondary use of the book.

I also want to emphasize the need for lessons to be designed for success of students prior to implementation, hence the new banner across the pages related to a practical way to consider the concepts of Universal Design for Learning (UDL). If you are not familiar with this concept be certain to visit http://www.cast.org for more detailed information and ideas. Simply, the concept of UDL is to create lessons that fit all students from the beginning instead of later retrofitting the lesson based upon specific needs.

Therefore, after planning a lesson with your co-teacher, I recommend you end your planning either in person or separately if time is limited, checking off each of the boxes at the top of the page on the right hand side of the lesson plans. A universally designed lesson provides multiple ways for students to express, engage and represent the "big idea" of the lesson. I have found in helping co-teaching teams plan for a UDL structure that if each lesson passes the test for the following students, then your co-taught plan is probably designed in a proactive manner to meet the needs of the range of learners in your classroom not only today but probably the ones you will have in future years on this same topic. Keep in mind if you are in a state that has adopted the common core standards, if you can get it right the first time with the common core for all students, this approach will save considerable amounts of time in the future.

So I recommend after you both have completed your plans to check off the boxes related to your lesson being ready for the following needs in your classroom. For any box you can't check-off today perhaps each of you could think about that specific need either throughout the lesson or during your own separate reflection time.

Walk
Talk
See
Hear
Behave
Learn the way you traditionally teach

I also have added several co-teaching assessment tools you might want to use in the classroom as well as updated the references on the plethora of articles that are out there on both co-teaching and inclusion.These tools I recommend you use to bring co-teaching to what I consider to be the highest level, which is when in the co-taught classroom, the IEP becomes a living and breathing document. These tools are provided for you to consider using to address a range of needs in the classroom as well as to assess student learning.

To assist you in trying to stay up-to-date on the infinite number of useful web sites, I maintain a Delicious site (http://www.delicious.com/ldieker) with links to over 200 great web sites that teachers across the country have shared with me. I'm sure you will discover valuable resources for your classroom by browing my Delicious list.

Best wishes for a successful and rewarding co-teaching experience!

Five Tools For Every Co-taught Classroom

1. Co-teaching Backpacks

Consider having a backpack filled with tools that you can use to enhance the role of the learning or behavioral specialists in the classroom along with making the lesson more universally designed.

This list is just an example of what you might want to have in the backpack:
- solo plastic plates
- low odor dry erase markers
- wiki stix
- talking calculator
- clipboard
- paper
- graph paper
- golf pencils
- pencil grips
- fun writing pens
- erasable highlighters
- koosh ball (2)
- stress ball (2)
- Teach timers
- Vibrating watch
- Livescribe pen
- Video recording device

2. Clipboard Checklist

Use a clipboard and one of these two checklists to collect data to monitor student performance. One is for assessing the way you met a range of learners' needs and the other is to gather data on the "big idea" for the day.

Use this **Multiple Intelligence Checklist** as you move about the classroom to ensure you have addressed a range of learning needs. At the end of class do a quick reflection on the various types of intelligence and any you missed. Consider using something based on that type of intelligence to open the lesson the next day.

Type of Intelligence	Check if address and if not list a way to reinforce the big idea through this type of intelligence
naturalistic	☐
musical	☐
Logical-mathematical	☐
existential	☐
interpersonal	☐
Bodily-kinesthetic	☐
Linguistic	☐
Intra-personal	☐
spatial	☐

Use this **IEP observation Checklist** to write summaries of students' IEP goals on the left side and names across the top. Then when students are in the co-taught setting, both teachers can jot down ideas on the clipboard to having ongoing data collection to make IEP goals living and breathing in your co-taught settings. The example below illustrates how a paraprofessional might gather data and do targeted interventions. The para can work on any area listed but the students highlighted he is to take data on their progress towards these goals this week. Also there is a note from the special educator about a specific target area for one other student at the bottom. This type of tool allows the paraprofessional to be in a co-taught classroom but with a clear role as to his or her role.

IEP Objective	Sydney	Rashan	Tabby	Lenore	Noah	Dan	Annie
Speak at least twice on topic each class	*	*	*				
Answer a teacher question	*	*	*				*
Raise hand to participate					*	*	
Complete at least 50% of the classroom assignment					*	*	
Complete at least 80% of the classroom assignment	*	*	*	*			
Write assignment in planner					*	*	
Complete 2 step directions the first time given					*	*	
Compare 2 concepts verbally or in writing		*	*				*
Participates in group by taking role assigned in cooperative learning					*	*	
Contributes to cooperative group					*	*	
Comprehends higher level questions (represented by oral or written response)	*						(
NOTES about students overall performance this day							Annie has cried three times this week and mom is worried please let me know if you see any change in her behavior.

3. Timer

Think about using a timer in the following ways to enhance your co-teaching:
- Set it every 8-10 minutes to make sure you use a brain break and let the other teacher lead that break in different type of multiple intelliegence
- Use it to give yourself some space from a student who might be on your last nerve (I like to call this putting myself in timeout).
- Use it to have the teacher who enters the other teacher's room to do a 5 minute opening – set the timer as a gentle reminder as to when it is time to "get off the stage"
- Use it to time when you are to switch roles
- Use it to break up a 20 minute block for a group activity. Instead set the timer with clear expectations academically and behaviorally that students are to meet every 7 minutes.
- Use it for quiet time activities
- Use it to ensure that you allow adequate processing time for student talk instead of teacher talk. Remember just because there are 2 teachers in the room there should not be increased talking but these 2 teachers should be used to increase student talk.

4. Brain Breaks

Explore these activities as a way of providing students with a brief brain break.

Activity	More Activities
Stand up/sit down	Look out the window and relate an image or cloud to our concepts
Draw a picture	Use your body to show a particular concept – (e.g., action verb, etc.)
Write a newspaper paragraph summarizing what we have taught so far	Go to a website to show an image
Use your wiki stik to make an image	Share a cartoon to support your point
Send a tweet to summarize our points	Write down 3 main points so far today – compare your list to your neighbors
Make a 30 second rap of our work	Come to the board with a peer and write 2 words and 2 images
Tell a neighbor your thoughts on the topic	20 questions
Find a passage in the book related to …	Summarize in 10 words or less and a peer counts that you used less than 10 words (keep trying until you get it)
Use the whiteboard to show 2 words and 2 images	Show your answer on a dry erase board or solo plastic plate
Walk until the music stops and then talk with the student closest on your right	Find 2 things in the room that relate to the concept being discussed
Watch a youtube video to support the concept	Chant 5 times the main idea
Ask students to talk about their favorite movie and relate it to the topic	On a post it note write a one sentence summary of each of the 5 pages read so far

5. The Co-Planner

Of course the co-planner. Keep a copy of the lesson plan on your clipboard so as you enter the room you can do quick sidebar discussions to ensure nothing in the lesson has changed. Also this tool is great to use to keep data that you can refer back to during IEP, RTI or parent meetings.

Sample Co-Teaching Lesson Plans

Note: Below are sample lesson plans to illustrate how the co-teaching planning model can be used across subject areas. In contrast to typical plan books, this co-planner is designed for those periods in which two educators co-teach.

Week of _____

Subject _____

Class Hour _____

Strategy Suggestion...

Target Students
_____
_____
_____
_____
_____

Day/Date	Big Idea/Goals	Lesson Activities	Assessment	
			Standard	**Adapted/Modified**
Language Arts	**All / Some** All students will prepare an oral presentation on a book of their choice. Some students will evaluate peers' presentations and provide one constructive comment and one positive comment.	Review book report requirements. Provide students in-class time to prepare report.	5 minute oral presentation with a clear sequence of ideas. Complete evaluations with a minimum of 1 positive and 1 constructive comment.	Provides pictures and 1 sentence statement of each picture. Give verbal positive comment to at least one peer following the presentation.
Algebra	**All / Some** All students will multiply the correct terms in a binomial and combine two binomials into a single binomial. All students will use positive language with their peers. Some students will explain how to multiply binominals to a peer.	Demonstrate the FOIL method. Assign practice problems for students to complete.	**Standard** Homework of 20 problems with 90% accuracy. Make at least 1 positive comment during class today.	**Adapted/Modified** Complete 5 problems with 80% accuracy. Respond with an affirmation to at least one positive comment made by a peer (e.g., thank you).
Science	**All / Some** All students will be able to use a balance. All students will demonstrate appropriate cooperative group behavior. Some students will extrapolate information from observation/data collection.	Students will gather necessary materials (balance, weights, etc.) for the experiment. As a team, students will balance various objects and record data on an observation form.	**Standard** Complete data sheet for balancing 10 items with 90% accuracy. Peer rating of 4/5 on contribution to group.	**Adapted/Modified** Complete data sheet for balancing 5 items with 80% accuracy. Peer rating of 3 or higher on contribution to group.

This page is designed to be completed by Educator One.

Sample Co-Teaching Lesson Plans

Co-Teaching Structures:
- (O) one lead, one support
- (S) station teaching
- (P) parallel teaching
- (A) alternative teaching
- (T) team teaching

Strategy Suggestion...

Students with Special Needs

Co-Teaching Structure	Academic Adaptations (as needed for gifted students and students with disabilities)	Behavioral Adaptations	Materials/ Support Needed	Performance Data and Notes
Alternative teaching	• Allow students to present report using a variety of styles (brown bag report, rap song, note cards, etc.) • Allow students with language issues to present with a peer. • Allow three minute presentations for Sue and Jason.	• Review behavior expectations of audience; provide student with specific checklist to self-monitor behavior.	Provide small group break out sessions to edit, practice, refine, etc.	*We need to talk about Tanya's performance this past week.*
One teach– one support	William will complete one-half of the assignment. Zoe will identify terms for each FOIL.	When frustrated, Alex will be allowed two-minute breaks to regain composure.	Color code FOIL terms. Teacher observation.	*I am worried about too much support for Sally. She does not seem to be learning to work independently.*
Parallel instruction. Monitor students working in collaborative teams.	Jeff and Zoe will be required to record list of materials used. Given a list of objects, Kevin will circle pictures of materials used in lab.	Jerrod's teammates will ask him 5 questions during lab. David will pass out lab materials.	Teacher generated picture worksheet. Peer coaching training.	*IEP goal: When asked a question, student 4 will respond 70% of the time by answering yes or no.* *Remember to record more data on this IEP goal.*

This page is designed to be completed by Educator Two.

As You Begin...

Meeting Agenda
Suggested time: 3 hours

Before you start the new school year I strongly recommend spending, at a minimum, half a day together talking over the following questions:

1. How will we deal with any behavioral issues that arise?

2. How will we deal with grading?

3. Who will contact parents and how will we share and maintain communication throughout the year?

4. Are there accommodations that students will be allowed to use in local and state assessments that we need to incorporate into our daily planning?

Reflective Framework

Here are some questions to guide the development of your classroom structure to ensure the success of both teachers and your students:

1. What do we see as our roles in the classrooms?
2. What do we see as our individual strengths in what we will contribute to all learners?
3. What are our pet peeves about teaching?
4. Will we share teaching space or are there two desk available in the room? If shared, how do we plan to share supplies, passes, and basic materials?
5. When will we have time to plan together?
6. What rules do we want to set related to any planning time we might have? For example, can we agree:
    a. To talk about students individually after we plan for the entire class.
    b. To make certain we arrive at our assigned time promptly with needed materials to make the most use of limited time together.
    c. To create a Plan B about what to do if one of us is out or cannot plan.
7. What if our designated time together is not enough time to plan our lessons effectively? How will we proceed?
8. What is the best thing we anticipate will result from our work together this year?
9. What is our greatest fear about working as a team?
10. How do we plan to introduce ourselves the first day of class?
11. How do we plan to handle any issues of fairness that might arise in the class?

Topics to revisit in our next meeting...

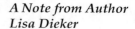

A Note from Author Lisa Dieker

One issue many co-teaching teams fail to address involves informing parents of the new service delivery model in which both general and special education students will be receiving services.

As you begin your planning for the new school year, remember to take time to prepare a letter that you can send home informing parents that their child will receive the benefit of two teachers in your class this year.

Professional Development Resources

Dieker, L. (2013). *Demystifying secondary inclusion* (2nd ed). NY: National Professional Resources, Inc.

Mastropieri, M. A., Scruggs, T. E., Graetz, J., Norland, J., Gardizi, W., & McDuffie, K. (2005). Case studies in co-teaching in the content areas: Successes, failures, and challenges. *Intervention in School and Clinic*, 40(5), 260-270.

Rubistar
http://rubistar.4teachers.org/

Internet4Classrooms
http://www.internet4classrooms.com/

Follow-up To-Do List
Educator 1

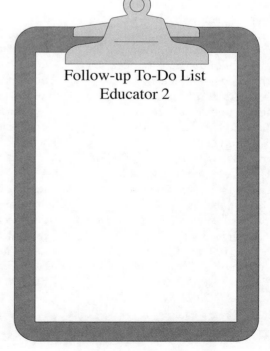

Follow-up To-Do List
Educator 2

Selected References to Research on Co-Teaching

Austin, V. L. (2001). Teachers' beliefs about co-teaching. *Remedial and Special Education, 22,* 245-255.

Bacharach, N., Heck, T., & Dahlberg, K. (2008). Co-teaching in higher education. *Journal of College Teaching and Learning, 5*(3), 9-16.

Boyle, C., Topping, K., Jindal-Snape, D., & Norwich, B. (2011). The importance of peer-support for teaching staff when including children with special educational needs. *School Psychology International, 33*(2), 167-184.

Cook, L., & Friend, M. P. (1995). Co-teaching: Guidelines for creating effective practices. *Focus on Exceptional Children, 28*(3), 1-16.

Cozart, A.C., Cudahy, D., Ndunda, M., & Van Sickle, M. (2003). The challenges of co-teaching within a multicultural context. *Multicultural Education, 10,* 43-45.

Cramer, E., & Nevin, A. (2006). A mixed methodology analysis of co-teacher assessments. *Teacher Education and Special Education, 29*(4), 261-274.

Cramer, E., Liston, A., Nevin, A., & Thousand, J. (2010). Co-teaching in urban secondary school districts to meet the needs of all teachers and learners: Implications for teacher education reform. *International Journal of Whole Schooling, 6*(2), 59-76.

Damore, S. J., & Murray, C. (2009). Urban elementary school teachers' perspectives regarding collaborative teaching practices. *Remedial and Special Education, 30*(4), 234-244.

Dieker, L. (1998). Rationale for co-teaching. *Social Studies Review, 37*(2), 62-65.

Dieker, L. A. (2001). What are the characteristics of "effective" middle and high school co-taught teams for students with disabilities? *Preventing School Failure, 46*(1), 14-23.

Dieker, L. A. (2013). *Demystifying secondary inclusion* (2nd Ed). Port Chester, NY: National Professional Resources, Inc.

Dieker, L. A., & Berg, C. A. (2002). Can secondary math, science and special educators really work together? *Teacher Education and Special Education, 25,* 92-99.

Dieker, L. A., & Hines, R. (2012). *Guide to teaching all content effectively in the inclusive secondary classroom.* Upper Saddle, NJ: Pearson.

Dieker, L.A., & Murawski, W.W. (2003). Co-teaching at the secondary level: Unique issues, current trends, and suggestions for success. *The High School Journal, 86*(4), 1-13.

Duchaine, E. L., Jolivette, K., Fredrick, L. D., (2011). The effect of teacher coaching with performance feedback on behavior-specific praise in inclusion classrooms. *Education and Treatment of Children, 34*(2), 209-227.

Friend, M., & Cook, L. (2007). *Interactions: Collaboration skills for school professionals* (5th ed.). Boston, MA: Allyn & Bacon.

Gable, R.A., Mostert, M.P., & Tonelson, S.W. (2004). Assessing professional collaboration in schools: Knowing what works. *Preventing School Failure, 48*(3), 4-8.

Hang, Q., & Rabren, K. (2009). An examination of co-teaching: Perspectives and efficacy indicators. *Remedial & Special Education, 30*(5), 259-268.

Harbort, G., Gunter, P.L., Hull, K., Brown, Q., Venn, M.L., Wiley, L.P., & Wiley, E.W. (2007). Behaviors of teachers in co-taught classes in a secondary school. *Teacher Education and Special Education, 30*(1), 13-23.

Hughes, C. E., & Murawski, W. W. (2001). Lessons from another field: Applying co-teaching strategies to gifted education. *Gifted Child Quarterly, 45*(3), 195-204.

Keefe, E. B., & Moore, V. (2004). The challenge of co-teaching in inclusive classrooms at the high school level: What the teachers told us. *American Secondary Education, 32*(3), 77-88.

Kim, A. H., Woodruff, A. L., Klein, C., & Vaughn, S. (2006). Facilitating co-teaching for literacy in general education classrooms through technology: Focus on students with learning disabilities. *Reading and Writing Quarterly, 22*(3), 269-291.

Kohler-Evans, P. A. (2006). Co-teaching: How to make this marriage work in front of the kids. *Education, 127,* 260-264.

Little, M., & Dieker, L. A. (2009). Co-Teaching: Challenges and solutions for administrators. *Principal Leadership, 9*(8), 42-46.

Luckner, J. (1999). An examination of the two co-teaching classrooms. *American Annals of the Deaf, 144*(1), 24-34.

Magiera, K., & Zigmond, N. (2005). Co-teaching in middle school classrooms under routine conditions: Does the instructional experience differ for students with disabilities in co-taught and solo-taught classes? *Learning Disabilities Research & Practice, 20*(2), 79-85.

Magiera, K., Smith, C., Zigmond, N., & Gebauer, K. (2005). Benefits of co-teaching in secondary mathematics classes.

Selected References to Research on Co-Teaching

Teaching Exceptional Children, 37(3), 20-24.

Magiera, K.A., & Simmons, R.J. (2005). *The Magiera-Simmons quality indicator model of co-teaching*. Fredonia, NY: Excelsior Educational Service.

Mastropieri, M., Scruggs, T., Graetz, J., Norland, J., Gardizi, W., & McDuffie, K. (2005). Case studies in co-teaching in the content areas: Successes, failures, and challenges. *Intervention in School & Clinic, 40*(5), 260-270.

Mastropieri, M., Scruggs, T., Norland, J., Berkeley, S., McDuffie, K., et al. (2006). Differentiated curriculum enhancement in inclusive middle school science: Effects on classroom and high-stakes tests. *Journal of Special Education, 40*(3), 130-137.

McDuffie, K.,Mastropieri, M.A., & Scruggs, T.E. (2009). Promoting success in content area classes: Is value added through co-teaching? *Exceptional Children, 75*, 493-510.

McLeskey, J., & Waldron, N. (2002). School change and inclusive schools: Lessons learned from practice. *Phi Delta Kappan, 84*(1), 65-72.

Murawski, W. W. (2006). Student outcomes in co-taught secondary English classes: How can we improve? *Reading and Writing Quarterly, 22*(3) 227-247.

Murawski, W. W. (2009). *Collaborative teaching in secondary schools: Making the co- teaching marriage work!* Thousand Oaks, CA: Corwin Press.

Murawski, W. W. (2012). 10 tips for using co-planning time more efficiently. *Teaching Exceptional Children, 44*(4), 8-15.

Murawski, W. W., & Dieker, L. A. (2004). Tips and strategies for co-teaching at the secondary level. *Teaching Exceptional Children, 36*(5), 52-58.

Murawski, W. W., & Hughes, C. E. (2009). Response to Intervention, collaboration, and co-teaching: A necessary combination for successful systemic change. *Preventing School Failure, 53*(4), 67-77.

Murawski, W. W., & Swanson, H. L. (2001). A meta-analysis of co-teaching research: Where are the data? *Remedial and Special Education, 22*(5), 258-267.

Murawski, W., & Lochner, W. (2011). Observing co-teaching: What to ask for, look for, and listen for. *Intervention in School and Clinic, 46*(3), 174-183.

Murawski, W.W. (2010). *Collaborative teaching in elementary schools: Making the co- teaching marriage work!* Thousand Oaks, CA: Corwin Press.

Nevin, A., Cramer, E., Voigt, J., & Salazar, L. (2008). Instructional modifications, adaptations, and accommodations of co-teachers who loop: A descriptive case study. *Teacher Education and Special Education, 31*(4), 283-297.

Nichols, J., Dowdy, A., & Nichols, C. (2010). Co-teaching: An educational promise for children with disabilities or a quick fix to meet the mandates of No Child Left Behind? *Education, 130*(4), 647-651.

Noonan, M. J., McCormick, L., & Heck, R. H. (2003). The co-teacher relationship scale: Applications for professional development. *Education and Training in Developmental Disabilities, 38*, 113-120.

Pearl, C. A., Dieker, L. A. & Kirkpatrick, R. (2012). A five-year retrospective on Arkansas Department of Education co-teaching project. *Professional Development in Education, 39*, 1-17.

Ploessl, D., Rock, M., Schoenfeld, N., & Blanks, B. (2010). On the same page: Practical techniques to enhance co-teaching interactions. *Intervention in School & Clinic, 45*(3), 158-168.

Scruggs, T., Mastropieri, M., & McDuffie, K.A. (2007). Co-teaching in inclusive classrooms: A metasynthesis of qualitative research. *Exceptional Children, 73*(4), 392-416.

Sileo, J., & van Garderen, D. (2010). Creating optimal opportunities to learn mathematics: Blending co-teaching structures with research-based practices. *Teaching Exceptional Children, 42*(3), 14-21.

Thousand, J. S., Villa, R. A., & Nevin, A. I. (2008). The many faces of collaborative planning and teaching. *Theory into Practice, 45*(3), 239-248.

Villa, R., Thousand, J. & Nevin, A. (2008). *A guide to co-teaching: Practical tips for facilitating student learning* (2nd ed). Thousand Oaks, CA: Corwin Press.

Wilson, G. (2005). This doesn't look familiar! A supervisor's guide for observing co-teachers. *Intervention in School & Clinic, 40*(5), 271-275.

Wischnowski, M., Salmon, S., & Eaton, K. (2004). Evaluating co-teaching as a means for successful inclusion of students with disabilities in a rural district. *Rural Special Education Quarterly, 23*(3), 3-14.

Week of _____

Subject _____

Class Hour _____

Strategy Suggestion...
Get acquainted activities – Use these types of activities regularly to help students learn about each other. These types of activities are critical if students with disabilities join the class in the middle of a quarter.

Target Students
_____
_____
_____
_____

Does your overall lesson meet the needs of students who cannot ...

Day/Date	Big Idea/Goals	Lesson Activities	Assessment	
			Standard	Adapted/Modified
Monday	All / Some			
Tuesday	All / Some			
Wednesday	All / Some			
Thursday	All / Some			
Friday	All / Some			

This page is designed to be completed by Educator One

Co-Teaching Structures:
(O) one lead, one support
(S) station teaching
(P) parallel teaching
(A) alternative teaching
(T) team teaching

Students with Special Needs
_____
_____
_____
_____
_____

☐ Walk ☐ Talk ☐ See ☐ Hear ☐ Behave or ☐ Learn the way you traditionally teach?

Co-Teaching Structure	Academic Adaptations (as needed for gifted students and students with disabilities)	Behavioral Adaptations	Materials/ Support Needed	Performance Data and Notes

This page is designed to be completed by Educator Two.

Week of _____

Subject _____

Class Hour _____

Target Students
_____
_____
_____
_____
_____

Does your overall lesson meet the needs of students who cannot ...

Day/Date	Big Idea/Goals	Lesson Activities	Assessment	
			Standard	Adapted/Modified
Monday	All / Some			
Tuesday	All / Some			
Wednesday	All / Some			
Thursday	All / Some			
Friday	All / Some			

This page is designed to be completed by Educator On

Co-Teaching Structures:
- (O) one lead, one support
- (S) station teaching
- (P) parallel teaching
- (A) alternative teaching
- (T) team teaching

Students with Special Needs
_____
_____
_____
_____
_____
_____

☐ Walk ☐ Talk ☐ See ☐ Hear ☐ Behave or ☐ Learn the way you traditionally teach?

Co-Teaching Structure	Academic Adaptations (as needed for gifted students and students with disabilities)	Behavioral Adaptations	Materials/ Support Needed	Performance Data and Notes

This page is designed to be completed by Educator Two.

Week of _____

Subject _____

Class Hour _____

Strategy Suggestion...
Role plays – Incorporate role plays into your lessons that illustrate appropriate social skills for solving problems with peers.

Target Students

_____
_____
_____
_____
_____

Does your overall lesson meet the needs of students who cannot ...

Day/Date	Big Idea/Goals	Lesson Activities	Assessment	
			Standard	Adapted/Modified
Monday	All / Some			
Tuesday	All / Some			
Wednesday	All / Some			
Thursday	All / Some			
Friday	All / Some			

This page is designed to be completed by Educator On..

-16-

Co-Teaching Structures:
- (O) one lead, one support
- (S) station teaching
- (P) parallel teaching
- (A) alternative teaching
- (T) team teaching

Students with Special Needs
_____
_____
_____
_____
_____

☐ Walk ☐ Talk ☐ See ☐ Hear ☐ Behave or ☐ Learn the way you traditionally teach?

Co-Teaching Structure	Academic Adaptations (as needed for gifted students and students with disabilities)	Behavioral Adaptations	Materials/ Support Needed	Performance Data and Notes

This page is designed to be completed by Educator Two.

Week of _____

Subject _____

Class Hour _____

Target Students
_____
_____
_____
_____
_____

Does your overall lesson meet the needs of students who cannot ...

Day/Date	Big Idea/Goals	Lesson Activities	Assessment	
			Standard	Adapted/Modified
Monday	All / Some			
Tuesday	All / Some			
Wednesday	All / Some			
Thursday	All / Some			
Friday	All / Some			

This page is designed to be completed by Educator One

Co-Teaching Structures:
(O) one lead, one support
(S) station teaching
(P) parallel teaching
(A) alternative teaching
(T) team teaching

Strategy Suggestion...
Teach social skills – Write a goal on the board for the day or week (e.g., use positive language) and reward and praise students when they exhibit the skill.

Students with Special Needs
_____
_____
_____
_____
_____

☐ Walk ☐ Talk ☐ See ☐ Hear ☐ Behave or ☐ Learn the way you traditionally teach?

Co-Teaching Structure	Academic Adaptations (as needed for gifted students and students with disabilities)	Behavioral Adaptations	Materials/ Support Needed	Performance Data and Notes

This page is designed to be completed by Educator Two.

Week 4 Co-Teaching Progress Check-up

Meeting Agenda
Suggested time: 30 minutes

Now is a good time to schedule a meeting between co-teachers to reflect on the experience to-date. Use the following agenda to guide the discussion.

1. Discuss each of the questions in the Reflective Framework (below).

2. Read and discuss the Author's Note (next page).

3. Record your thoughts and notes in the space provided for
   - Ideas
   - Topics to revisit in our next meeting
   - Follow-up to-do list for each team member

Reflective Framework

Co-Teaching (Dieker, 2006)

- How will you determine the success of the co-teaching relationship? (i.e., students' grades, personal perceptions, student/parent comments)

- How will you evaluate student learning? Take time now and write a date on the calendar for your next meeting. I recommend meeting at least once a month.

- How will you conduct these evaluations? (i.e., talk in person, send written notes, meet outside of school)

- How will you determine the students' perceptions of co-teaching each semester? (i.e., informational evaluation, interviews)

- How will you keep your administrator involved in the process and assist him/her in evaluating your co-teaching efforts? (i.e., written notes, informal observations, team meetings)

- How will you involve parents in all aspects of the co-teaching relationship? (i.e., letters home, phone conversations, parent meetings)

Topics to revisit in our next meeting...

A Note from Author Lisa Dieker

A simple rule to determine your success in your co-teaching relationship is to answer two questions: (1) Is this co-teaching relationship good for us? (2) Is the co-teaching relationship good for ALL students?

If the answers to both questions are "yes," then you should continue to develop and refine your co-teaching relationship.

If the answers are something other than "yes," then how will you address the issues? Or, do you need to find a different service delivery model to insure success?

Professional Development Resources

Hang, Q., & Rabren, K. (2009). An examination of co-teaching: Perspectives and efficacy indicators. *Remedial and Special Education*, 30(5), 259-268.

Cramer, E., Liston, A., Nevin, A., & Thousand, J. (2010). Co-teaching in urban secondary school districts to meet the needs of all teachers and learners: Implications for teacher education reform. *International Journal of Whole Schooling*, 6(2), 59-76.

Iris Center
http://iris.peabody.vanderbilt.edu/

Toondoo.com
http://www.toondoo.com/

Follow-up To-Do List
Educator 1

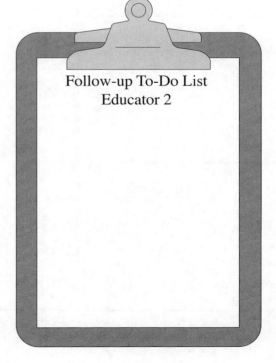

Follow-up To-Do List
Educator 2

Week of _____

Subject _____

Class Hour _____

Target Students
_____
_____
_____
_____
_____

Does your overall lesson meet the needs of students who cannot ...

Day/Date	Big Idea/Goals	Lesson Activities	Assessment	
			Standard	Adapted/Modified
Monday	All / Some			
Tuesday	All / Some			
Wednesday	All / Some			
Thursday	All / Some			
Friday	All / Some			

This page is designed to be completed by Educator One

Co-Teaching Structures:
- (O) one lead, one support
- (S) station teaching
- (P) parallel teaching
- (A) alternative teaching
- (T) team teaching

Students with Special Needs

_____
_____
_____
_____
_____
_____

☐ Walk ☐ Talk ☐ See ☐ Hear ☐ Behave or ☐ Learn the way you traditionally teach?

Co-Teaching Structure	Academic Adaptations (as needed for gifted students and students with disabilities)	Behavioral Adaptations	Materials/ Support Needed	Performance Data and Notes

This page is designed to be completed by Educator Two.

-23-

Week of _____

Subject _____

Class Hour _____

Strategy Suggestion...
Assign class roles – Give students roles such as captain, co-captain, recorder, sunshine person, etc. Be certain students with disabilities have the chance to serve in leadership roles.

Target Students
_____
_____
_____
_____
_____

Does your overall lesson meet the needs of students who cannot ...

Day/Date	Big Idea/Goals	Lesson Activities	Assessment	
			Standard	Adapted/Modified
Monday	All / Some			
Tuesday	All / Some			
Wednesday	All / Some			
Thursday	All / Some			
Friday	All / Some			

This page is designed to be completed by Educator One

Co-Teaching Structures:
- (O) one lead, one support
- (S) station teaching
- (P) parallel teaching
- (A) alternative teaching
- (T) team teaching

Students with Special Needs
_____
_____
_____
_____
_____
_____
_____

☐ Walk ☐ Talk ☐ See ☐ Hear ☐ Behave or ☐ Learn the way you traditionally teach?

Co-Teaching Structure	Academic Adaptations (as needed for gifted students and students with disabilities)	Behavioral Adaptations	Materials/ Support Needed	Performance Data and Notes

This page is designed to be completed by Educator Two.

Week of _____

Subject _____

Class Hour _____

Target Students
_____
_____
_____
_____

Does your overall lesson meet the needs of students who cannot ...

Day/Date	Big Idea/Goals	Lesson Activities	Assessment	
			Standard	Adapted/Modified
Monday	All / Some			
Tuesday	All / Some			
Wednesday	All / Some			
Thursday	All / Some			
Friday	All / Some			

This page is designed to be completed by Educator One

Co-Teaching Structures:
(O) one lead, one support
(S) station teaching
(P) parallel teaching
(A) alternative teaching
(T) team teaching

Students with Special Needs
_____
_____
_____
_____
_____
_____

☐ Walk ☐ Talk ☐ See ☐ Hear ☐ Behave or ☐ Learn the way you traditionally teach?

Co-Teaching Structure	Academic Adaptations (as needed for gifted students and students with disabilities)	Behavioral Adaptations	Materials/ Support Needed	Performance Data and Notes

This page is designed to be completed by Educator Two.

Week of _____

Subject _____

Class Hour _____

Strategy Suggestion...
Excuse book - Ask students to share their excuse for missing work by writing in an excuse notebook. When they have three excuses, contact their parents/guardian to let them know of the missing work.

Target Students
_____
_____
_____
_____
_____

Does your overall lesson meet the needs of students who cannot ...

Day/Date	Big Idea/Goals	Lesson Activities	Assessment	
			Standard	Adapted/Modified
Monday	All / Some			
Tuesday	All / Some			
Wednesday	All / Some			
Thursday	All / Some			
Friday	All / Some			

This page is designed to be completed by Educator One

Co-Teaching Structures:

(O) one lead, one support
(S) station teaching
(P) parallel teaching
(A) alternative teaching
(T) team teaching

Students with Special Needs

_____
_____
_____
_____
_____
_____

☐ Walk ☐ Talk ☐ See ☐ Hear ☐ Behave or ☐ Learn the way you traditionally teach?

Co-Teaching Structure	Academic Adaptations (as needed for gifted students and students with disabilities)	Behavioral Adaptations	Materials/ Support Needed	Performance Data and Notes

This page is designed to be completed by Educator Two.

Week 8 Co-Teaching Progress Check-up

Meeting Agenda
Suggested time: 30 minutes

Now is a good time to schedule a meeting between co-teachers to reflect on the experience to-date. Use the following agenda to guide the discussion.

Ideas

1. Discuss each of the questions in the Reflective Framework (below).

2. Read and discuss the Author's Note (next page).

3. Record your thoughts and notes in the space provided for
   - Ideas
   - Topics to revisit in our next meeting
   - Follow-up to-do list for each team member

Reflective Framework

As the first quarter draws to a close, now is a good time for a conversation about cooperative teaching and grading. Use the following discussion questions to guide the conversation:

Cooperative Teaching (Dieker, 2006)
- Do we both feel comfortable in our roles in the classroom today?
- What were the successes of today's lesson?
- What do we both see as areas that need to be addressed in future lessons?
- Who will be responsible for implementing these changes?
- Was consensus reached with regards to the final decision?
- Are there any collaborative issues that we should address to improve our collaborative relationship? (i.e., time, grading, role clarification, parental contact, assessment, etc.)

Grading (adapted from Meltzer, et al, 1996)
- Are you explicit about the grading policy?
- Do you use multilevel grading?
- Do you give credit for participation?
- Do you evaluate students' performance in a variety of ways?
- Do you embrace multiple intelligences?
- Do you evaluate social skills?
- Do you both clearly understand your role in grading?
- Do you embrace multiple intelligences?
- Do students who will be evaluated using modified grading understand how their final grade will be determined?

Topics to revisit in our next meeting...

A Note from Author Lisa Dieker

At this point in the semester, evaluation and planning should be a natural part of the co-teaching process. Now is a critical time to consider if there are issues related to grading. Are all students passing the class? If all students are not being successful, what will you do to try and ensure all students' success? You might want to keep John Dewey's thoughts in mind as you try to make further accommodations, "Look not for fault in the child, but in the teaching of the child."

Professional Development Resources

Dieker, L. A., & Rodriguez, J. (2013). Enhancing secondary cotaught science and mathematics classrooms through collaboration. *Intervention in School and Clinic*, 49 (1), 46-53 doi:10.1177/1053451213480028

Thousand, J. S., Villa, R. A., & Nevin, A. I. (2008). The many faces of collaborative planning and teaching. *Theory into Practice*, 45(3), 239-248.

Sum Dog
http://www.sumdog.com/

Remind: Send messages to students
https://www.remind.com/

Follow-up To-Do List
Educator 1

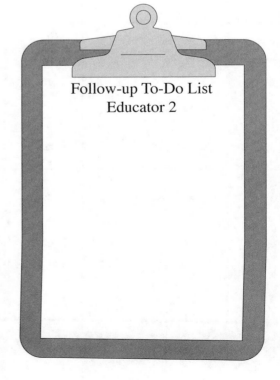

Follow-up To-Do List
Educator 2

Week of _____

Subject _____

Class Hour _____

Target Students
_____
_____
_____
_____
_____

Does your overall lesson meet the needs of students who cannot ...

Day/Date	Big Idea/Goals	Lesson Activities	Assessment	
			Standard	Adapted/Modified
Monday	All / Some			
Tuesday	All / Some			
Wednesday	All / Some			
Thursday	All / Some			
Friday	All / Some			

This page is designed to be completed by Educator One

Co-Teaching Structures:

(O) one lead, one support
(S) station teaching
(P) parallel teaching
(A) alternative teaching
(T) team teaching

Students with Special Needs

_____
_____
_____
_____
_____
_____

☐ Walk ☐ Talk ☐ See ☐ Hear ☐ Behave or ☐ Learn the way you traditionally teach?

Co-Teaching Structure	Academic Adaptations (as needed for gifted students and students with disabilities)	Behavioral Adaptations	Materials/ Support Needed	Performance Data and Notes

This page is designed to be completed by Educator Two.

Week of _____

Subject _____

Class Hour _____

Target Students
_____
_____
_____
_____
_____

Does your overall lesson meet the needs of students who cannot ...

Day/Date	Big Idea/Goals	Lesson Activities	Assessment	
			Standard	Adapted/Modified
Monday	All / Some			
Tuesday	All / Some			
Wednesday	All / Some			
Thursday	All / Some			
Friday	All / Some			

This page is designed to be completed by Educator One

Co-Teaching Structures:

(O) one lead, one support
(S) station teaching
(P) parallel teaching
(A) alternative teaching
(T) team teaching

Students with Special Needs

_____
_____
_____
_____
_____
_____

☐ Walk ☐ Talk ☐ See ☐ Hear ☐ Behave or ☐ Learn the way you traditionally teach?

Co-Teaching Structure	Academic Adaptations (as needed for gifted students and students with disabilities)	Behavioral Adaptations	Materials/ Support Needed	Performance Data and Notes

This page is designed to be completed by Educator Two.

Week of _____

Subject _____

Class Hour _____

Target Students
_____
_____
_____
_____

Does your overall lesson meet the needs of students who cannot ...

Day/Date	Big Idea/Goals	Lesson Activities	Assessment	
			Standard	Adapted/Modified
Monday	All / Some			
Tuesday	All / Some			
Wednesday	All / Some			
Thursday	All / Some			
Friday	All / Some			

This page is designed to be completed by Educator One

Co-Teaching Structures:

- (O) one lead, one support
- (S) station teaching
- (P) parallel teaching
- (A) alternative teaching
- (T) team teaching

Students with Special Needs

_____
_____
_____
_____
_____
_____

☐ Walk ☐ Talk ☐ See ☐ Hear ☐ Behave or ☐ Learn the way you traditionally teach?

Co-Teaching Structure	Academic Adaptations (as needed for gifted students and students with disabilities)	Behavioral Adaptations	Materials/ Support Needed	Performance Data and Notes

This page is designed to be completed by Educator Two.

Week of _____

Subject _____

Class Hour _____

Strategy Suggestion...
Conduct weekly study drills – Give students an assignment and give them 3 minutes to organize their materials. For the next 7 minutes have students start on their assignment; provide coaching and assistance as needed.

Target Students
_____
_____
_____
_____
_____

Does your overall lesson meet the needs of students who cannot ...

Day/Date	Big Idea/Goals	Lesson Activities	Assessment	
			Standard	Adapted/Modified
Monday	All / Some			
Tuesday	All / Some			
Wednesday	All / Some			
Thursday	All / Some			
Friday	All / Some			

This page is designed to be completed by Educator One

Co-Teaching Structures:

(O) one lead, one support
(S) station teaching
(P) parallel teaching
(A) alternative teaching
(T) team teaching

Strategy Suggestion...
Split page notes – Have students use the left side of their paper to jot down key points. Immediately after the lecture, give students a few minutes to fill in more specific details on the right side.

Students with Special Needs
_____
_____
_____
_____
_____

□ Walk □ Talk □ See □ Hear □ Behave or □ Learn the way you traditionally teach?

Co-Teaching Structure	Academic Adaptations (as needed for gifted students and students with disabilities)	Behavioral Adaptations	Materials/ Support Needed	Performance Data and Notes

This page is designed to be completed by Educator Two.

Week 12 Co-Teaching Progress Check-up

Meeting Agenda
Suggested time: 30 minutes

Now is a good time to schedule a meeting between co-teaching partners to reflect on the experience to-date. Use the following agenda to guide the discussion.

1. Discuss each of the questions in the Reflective Framework (below).

2. Read and discuss the Author's Note (next page).

3. Record your thoughts and notes in the space provided for
   - Ideas
   - Topics to revisit in our next meeting
   - Follow-up to-do list for each team member

Reflective Framework

For this month's meeting, now would be a good time to review your collaborative problem solving strategies. In the problem solving process, it is critical to recognize the outside influence on any problems that arise. Identify and select solutions that are within your power to implement. Use the following discussion questions to guide the conversation:

Problem Solving (Dieker & Monda-Amaya, 1996)

- What is the problem?

- What are the issues related to the problem?

- What factors beyond the classroom may have contributed to the problem?

- What solutions could be used to solve the problem?

- What can we do to solve the problem?

- What justification can we provide to support our solution(s)?

Topics to revisit in our next meeting...

Professional Development Resources

Conderman, G., & Hedin, L. (2012). Purposeful assessment practices for co-teachers. *Teaching Exceptional Children*, 44(4), 19-22.

Nichols, J., Dowdy, A., & Nichols, C. (2010). Co-teaching: An educational promise for children with disabilities or a quick fix to meet the mandates of No Child Left Behind? *Education*, 130(4), 647-651.

Tool of the Week
http://www.tooloftheweek.org/

Socrative (all students can respond using any device)
http://socrative.com/

Follow-up To-Do List
Educator 1

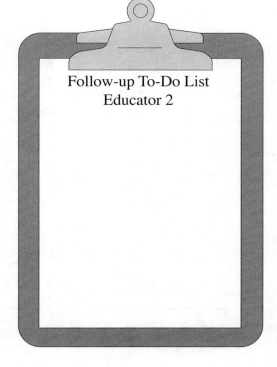

Follow-up To-Do List
Educator 2

Week of _____

Subject _____

Class Hour _____

Target Students
_____
_____
_____
_____
_____

Does your overall lesson meet the needs of students who cannot ...

Day/Date	Big Idea/Goals	Lesson Activities	Assessment	
			Standard	Adapted/Modified
Monday	All / Some			
Tuesday	All / Some			
Wednesday	All / Some			
Thursday	All / Some			
Friday	All / Some			

This page is designed to be completed by Educator On‹

Co-Teaching Structures:

(O) one lead, one support

(S) station teaching

(P) parallel teaching

(A) alternative teaching

(T) team teaching

Students with Special Needs

_____

_____

_____

_____

_____

☐ Walk ☐ Talk ☐ See ☐ Hear ☐ Behave or ☐ Learn the way you traditionally teach?

Co-Teaching Structure	Academic Adaptations (as needed for gifted students and students with disabilities)	Behavioral Adaptations	Materials/ Support Needed	Performance Data and Notes

This page is designed to be completed by Educator Two.

Week of _____

Subject _____

Class Hour _____

Target Students
_____
_____
_____
_____
_____

Does your overall lesson meet the needs of students who cannot ...

Day/Date	Big Idea/Goals	Lesson Activities	Assessment	
			Standard	Adapted/Modified
Monday	All / Some			
Tuesday	All / Some			
Wednesday	All / Some			
Thursday	All / Some			
Friday	All / Some			

This page is designed to be completed by Educator One

-44-

Co-Teaching Structures:
(O) one lead, one support
(S) station teaching
(P) parallel teaching
(A) alternative teaching
(T) team teaching

Students with Special Needs
_____
_____
_____
_____
_____

☐ Walk ☐ Talk ☐ See ☐ Hear ☐ Behave or ☐ Learn the way you traditionally teach?

Co-Teaching Structure	Academic Adaptations (as needed for gifted students and students with disabilities)	Behavioral Adaptations	Materials/ Support Needed	Performance Data and Notes

This page is designed to be completed by Educator Two.

Week of _____

Subject _____

Class Hour _____

Strategy Suggestion...
Prereading techniques – Set a purpose, preview vocabulary, activate background knowledge, and relate background knowledge to new knowledge.

Target Students
_____
_____
_____
_____
_____

Does your overall lesson meet the needs of students who cannot ...

Day/Date	Big Idea/Goals	Lesson Activities	Assessment	
			Standard	Adapted/Modified
Monday	All / Some			
Tuesday	All / Some			
Wednesday	All / Some			
Thursday	All / Some			
Friday	All / Some			

This page is designed to be completed by Educator On[e]

Co-Teaching Structures:

(O) one lead, one support
(S) station teaching
(P) parallel teaching
(A) alternative teaching
(T) team teaching

Strategy Suggestion...
Skim, rap, and map – Skim text, rap about a section by forming questions from headings or titles, and map by creating a two-column chart.

Students with Special Needs
_____
_____
_____
_____
_____

☐ Walk ☐ Talk ☐ See ☐ Hear ☐ Behave or ☐ Learn the way you traditionally teach?

Co-Teaching Structure	Academic Adaptations (as needed for gifted students and students with disabilities)	Behavioral Adaptations	Materials/ Support Needed	Performance Data and Notes

This page is designed to be completed by Educator Two.

Week of _____

Subject _____

Class Hour _____

Strategy Suggestion...
Author's chair: Allow a student to be the author and answer questions from the students who are reading the book.

Target Students

_____
_____
_____
_____
_____

Does your overall lesson meet the needs of students who cannot ...

Day/Date	Big Idea/Goals	Lesson Activities	Assessment	
			Standard	Adapted/Modified
Monday	All / Some			
Tuesday	All / Some			
Wednesday	All / Some			
Thursday	All / Some			
Friday	All / Some			

This page is designed to be completed by Educator On‹

Co-Teaching Structures:

(O) one lead, one support
(S) station teaching
(P) parallel teaching
(A) alternative teaching
(T) team teaching

Students with Special Needs

_____
_____
_____
_____
_____
_____

□ Walk □ Talk □ See □ Hear □ Behave or □ Learn the way you traditionally teach?

Co-Teaching Structure	Academic Adaptations (as needed for gifted students and students with disabilities)	Behavioral Adaptations	Materials/ Support Needed	Performance Data and Notes

This page is designed to be completed by Educator Two.

Week 16 Co-Teaching Progress Check-up

Meeting Agenda
Suggested time: 30 minutes

Now is a good time to schedule a meeting between co-teaching partners to reflect on the experience to-date. Use the following agenda to guide the discussion.

1. Discuss each of the questions in the Reflective Framework (below).

2. Read and discuss the Author's Note (next page).

3. Record your thoughts and notes in the space provided for
   - Ideas
   - Topics to revisit in our next meeting
   - Follow-up to-do list for each team member

Reflective Framework

As the semester draws to a close, now would be a good time to carefully consider the success individual students have achieved this semester. As well as the success you have had in co-teaching. Rarely do students or others thank us but you can both thank each other for the amazing impact you have on children's lives. After sharing your appreciation, use the following discussion questions to guide the conversation:

Evaluation (Dieker, 2006)

   • Did we meet the needs of all students this semester?

   • Were there academic tasks/behaviors that we found difficult to deal with this semester?

   • Are there issues in which we need support in order to successfully meet the needs of all students?

   • Are there other students in which it would be beneficial for us to discuss how to effectively meet their needs?

Topics to revisit in our next meeting...

A Note from Author Lisa Dieker

Now is the time to assess the current co-taught classroom and to begin planning any needed changes for next semester. Here are some specific topics you may want to discuss:

- roles for each team member
- administrator involvement
- class composition
- grading
- ensuring IEPs for all students are being addressed
- additional resources needed

Professional Development Resources

Little, M., & Dieker, L. A. (2009). Co-Teaching: Challenges and solutions for administrators. *Principal Leadership*, 9(8), 42-46.

Sileo, J., & van Garderen, D. (2010). Creating optimal opportunities to learn mathematics: Blending co-teaching structures with research-based practices. *Teaching Exceptional Children*, 42(3), 14-21.

Learn Zillion
https://learnzillion.com/

News ELA
https://newsela.com/

Follow-up To-Do List
Educator 1

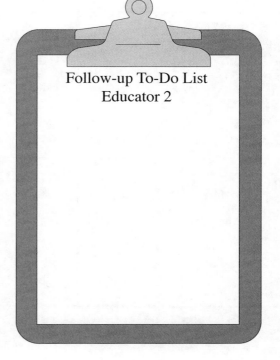

Follow-up To-Do List
Educator 2

Week of _____

Subject _____

Class Hour _____

Strategy Suggestion...
Predictions – Students work in pairs:
student reading a story predicts what will
happen, partner asks if prediction came
true, student reading offers a 10 word
summary; change roles.

Target Students

_____
_____
_____
_____
_____

Does your overall lesson meet the needs of students who cannot ...

Day/Date	Big Idea/Goals	Lesson Activities	Assessment	
			Standard	Adapted/Modified
Monday	All / Some			
Tuesday	All / Some			
Wednesday	All / Some			
Thursday	All / Some			
Friday	All / Some			

This page is designed to be completed by Educator On

Co-Teaching Structures:
- (O) one lead, one support
- (S) station teaching
- (P) parallel teaching
- (A) alternative teaching
- (T) team teaching

Strategy Suggestion...
Spirit reading – A student continues to read until the "spirit moves" them to stop and then any other student who the "spirit moves" can start reading.

Students with Special Needs
_____
_____
_____
_____
_____

☐ Walk ☐ Talk ☐ See ☐ Hear ☐ Behave or ☐ Learn the way you traditionally teach?

Co-Teaching Structure	Academic Adaptations (as needed for gifted students and students with disabilities)	Behavioral Adaptations	Materials/ Support Needed	Performance Data and Notes

This page is designed to be completed by Educator Two.

Week of _____

Subject _____

Class Hour _____

Strategy Suggestion...
Readability issues – When a text is just too difficult: provide the same content at an easier level, provide assistance with an organizer or study guide, or offer alternative formats (e.g., video, audio tape, pictures, computer).

Target Students
_____
_____
_____
_____
_____

Does your overall lesson meet the needs of students who cannot ...

Day/Date	Big Idea/Goals	Lesson Activities	Assessment	
			Standard	Adapted/Modified
Monday	All / Some			
Tuesday	All / Some			
Wednesday	All / Some			
Thursday	All / Some			
Friday	All / Some			

This page is designed to be completed by Educator On

Co-Teaching Structures:
- (O) one lead, one support
- (S) station teaching
- (P) parallel teaching
- (A) alternative teaching
- (T) team teaching

Students with Special Needs
_____
_____
_____
_____
_____
_____
_____

☐ Walk ☐ Talk ☐ See ☐ Hear ☐ Behave or ☐ Learn the way you traditionally teach?

Co-Teaching Structure	Academic Adaptations (as needed for gifted students and students with disabilities)	Behavioral Adaptations	Materials/ Support Needed	Performance Data and Notes

This page is designed to be completed by Educator Two.

Week of _____

Subject _____

Class Hour _____

Strategy Suggestion...
Draw a picture of the story – Student is asked to demonstrate comprehension by drawing a picture or pictograph of what they have read.

Target Students
_____
_____
_____
_____
_____

Does your overall lesson meet the needs of students who cannot ...

Day/Date	Big Idea/Goals	Lesson Activities	Assessment	
			Standard	Adapted/Modified
Monday	All / Some			
Tuesday	All / Some			
Wednesday	All / Some			
Thursday	All / Some			
Friday	All / Some			

This page is designed to be completed by Educator On

Co-Teaching Structures:

(O) one lead, one support
(S) station teaching
(P) parallel teaching
(A) alternative teaching
(T) team teaching

Strategy Suggestion...
Create a CD cover – Have students create a CD cover with song titles that reflect the key ideas in a chapter or story they have read.

Students with Special Needs

_____
_____
_____
_____
_____
_____

☐ Walk ☐ Talk ☐ See ☐ Hear ☐ Behave or ☐ Learn the way you traditionally teach?

Co-Teaching Structure	Academic Adaptations (as needed for gifted students and students with disabilities)	Behavioral Adaptations	Materials/ Support Needed	Performance Data and Notes

This page is designed to be completed by Educator Two.

Week of _____

Subject _____

Class Hour _____

Target Students
_____
_____
_____
_____
_____

Does your overall lesson meet the needs of students who cannot ...

Day/Date	Big Idea/Goals	Lesson Activities	Assessment	
			Standard	Adapted/Modified
Monday	All / Some			
Tuesday	All / Some			
Wednesday	All / Some			
Thursday	All / Some			
Friday	All / Some			

This page is designed to be completed by Educator On

Co-Teaching Structures:
- (O) one lead, one support
- (S) station teaching
- (P) parallel teaching
- (A) alternative teaching
- (T) team teaching

Strategy Suggestion...
Commercials – Have students write and videotape a commercial related to a book they have read.

☐ Walk ☐ Talk ☐ See ☐ Hear ☐ Behave or ☐ Learn the way you traditionally teach?

Co-Teaching Structure	Academic Adaptations (as needed for gifted students and students with disabilities)	Behavioral Adaptations	Materials/ Support Needed	Performance Data and Notes

This page is designed to be completed by Educator Two.

Week 20 Co-Teaching Progress Check-up

Meeting Agenda

Suggested time: 30 minutes

Now is a good time to schedule a meeting between co-teaching partners to reflect on the experience to-date. Use the following agenda to guide the discussion.

1. Discuss each of the questions in the Reflective Framework (below).

2. Read and discuss the Author's Note (next page).

3. Record your thoughts and notes in the space provided for
   - Ideas
   - Topics to revisit in our next meeting
   - Follow-up to-do list for each team member

Reflective Framework

As you reflect on the accommodations you have made, you may want to keep the following guidelines in mind:

- Have you shared the accommodations with parents so they can be reinforced at home?

- Are both teachers generating ideas?

- Are students asked to assess the value of the accommodations?

- Are the accommodations related to classroom tasks and the general education curriculum?

- Are these accommodations reasonable and still meet the needs of all students?

- Are these accommodations empowering rather than humiliating?

- Do students with disabilities have the opportunity to give as well as receive in your class?

Topics to revisit in our next meeting...

A Note from Author Lisa Dieker

At this point in the school year you may want to do a health checkup on your relationship as well as the accommodations being provided to students with disabilities. As the year progresses, it is critical to consider if you are providing each other with positive and productive energy in your relationship. For students, now is an excellent time to consider if accommodations are allowing enough independence and skills to prepare them for the next grade level.

Professional Development Resources

Murawski, W., & Lochner, W. (2011). Observing co-teaching: What to ask for, look for, and listen for. *Intervention in School and Clinic*, 46(3), 174-183.

Ploessl, D., Rock, M., Schoenfeld, N., & Blanks, B. (2010). On the same page: Practical techniques to enhance co-teaching interactions. *Intervention in School and Clinic*, 45(3), 158-168.

Apps for the Classroom
http://classwithapps.com/2013/06/tools-4-students/

Teaching Channel
https://www.teachingchannel.org/

Follow-up To-Do List
Educator 1

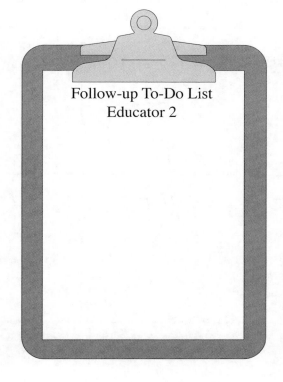

Follow-up To-Do List
Educator 2

Week of _____

Subject _____

Class Hour _____

Target Students
_____
_____
_____
_____
_____

Does your overall lesson meet the needs of students who cannot ...

Day/Date	Big Idea/Goals	Lesson Activities	Assessment	
			Standard	Adapted/Modified
Monday	All / Some			
Tuesday	All / Some			
Wednesday	All / Some			
Thursday	All / Some			
Friday	All / Some			

This page is designed to be completed by Educator One

Co-Teaching Structures:

(O) one lead, one support
(S) station teaching
(P) parallel teaching
(A) alternative teaching
(T) team teaching

Students with Special Needs
_____
_____
_____
_____
_____

☐ Walk ☐ Talk ☐ See ☐ Hear ☐ Behave or ☐ Learn the way you traditionally teach?

Co-Teaching Structure	Academic Adaptations (as needed for gifted students and students with disabilities)	Behavioral Adaptations	Materials/ Support Needed	Performance Data and Notes

This page is designed to be completed by Educator Two.

Week of _____

Subject _____

Class Hour _____

Strategy Suggestion...
Draw a Name – When reading aloud, students' names are drawn from a pile to ensure they are all paying attention. For a student with special needs, make arrangements with them ahead of time about the part they will read, and then be certain to call their name for the paragraph they have rehearsed.

Target Students

_____

_____

_____

_____

Does your overall lesson meet the needs of students who cannot ...

Day/Date	Big Idea/Goals	Lesson Activities	Assessment	
			Standard	Adapted/Modified
Monday	All / Some			
Tuesday	All / Some			
Wednesday	All / Some			
Thursday	All / Some			
Friday	All / Some			

This page is designed to be completed by Educator On

Co-Teaching Structures:

(O) one lead, one support
(S) station teaching
(P) parallel teaching
(A) alternative teaching
(T) team teaching

Strategy Suggestion...

KWL
  K = What you already Know
  W = What you Want to know
  L = What you Learned

Students with Special Needs

_____
_____
_____
_____
_____
_____

□ Walk □ Talk □ See □ Hear □ Behave or □ Learn the way you traditionally teach?

Co-Teaching Structure	Academic Adaptations (as needed for gifted students and students with disabilities)	Behavioral Adaptations	Materials/ Support Needed	Performance Data and Notes

This page is designed to be completed by Educator Two.

Week of _____

Subject _____

Class Hour _____

Strategy Suggestion...
Popcorn – Students read aloud and can say "popcorn" followed by the name of a peer in order to change readers.

Target Students
_____
_____
_____
_____
_____

Does your overall lesson meet the needs of students who cannot ...

Day/Date	Big Idea/Goals	Lesson Activities	Assessment	
			Standard	Adapted/Modified
Monday	All / Some			
Tuesday	All / Some			
Wednesday	All / Some			
Thursday	All / Some			
Friday	All / Some			

This page is designed to be completed by Educator On

Co-Teaching Structures:

(O) one lead, one support
(S) station teaching
(P) parallel teaching
(A) alternative teaching
(T) team teaching

Students with Special Needs

_____
_____
_____
_____
_____

☐ Walk ☐ Talk ☐ See ☐ Hear ☐ Behave or ☐ Learn the way you traditionally teach?

Co-Teaching Structure	Academic Adaptations (as needed for gifted students and students with disabilities)	Behavioral Adaptations	Materials/ Support Needed	Performance Data and Notes

This page is designed to be completed by Educator Two.

Week of _____

Subject _____

Class Hour _____

Target Students
_____
_____
_____
_____
_____

Does your overall lesson meet the needs of students who cannot ...

Day/Date	Big Idea/Goals	Lesson Activities	Assessment	
			Standard	Adapted/Modified
Monday	All / Some			
Tuesday	All / Some			
Wednesday	All / Some			
Thursday	All / Some			
Friday	All / Some			

This page is designed to be completed by Educator On

Co-Teaching Structures:
(O) one lead, one support
(S) station teaching
(P) parallel teaching
(A) alternative teaching
(T) team teaching

Students with Special Needs
_____
_____
_____
_____
_____
_____

☐ Walk ☐ Talk ☐ See ☐ Hear ☐ Behave or ☐ Learn the way you traditionally teach?

Co-Teaching Structure	Academic Adaptations (as needed for gifted students and students with disabilities)	Behavioral Adaptations	Materials/ Support Needed	Performance Data and Notes

This page is designed to be completed by Educator Two.

Week 24 Co-Teaching Progress Check-up

Meeting Agenda
Suggested time: 30 minutes

Now is a good time to schedule a meeting between co-teaching partners to reflect on the experience to-date. Use the following agenda to guide the discussion.

1. Discuss each of the questions in the Reflective Framework (below).

2. Read and discuss the Author's Note (next page).

3. Record your thoughts and notes in the space provided for
   - Ideas
   - Topics to revisit in our next meeting
   - Follow-up to-do list for each team member

Reflective Framework

Consider developing a matrix like the one below. The first column contains the IEP goals for a caseload of students. Across the top of the other columns are the names of the individual students. The dots illustrate that a specific goal is on the student's IEP and needs to be monitored in the co-taught setting. This type of matrix can be used by co-teachers to monitor students' progress toward goals and help focus planning for students' individual learning or behavior needs.

	Tom	Jim	Bill	Sue
Respects others and property	•			
Positive attitude/behavior related to teachers, peers	•	•		
Completes and submits homework as assigned	•		•	•
Brings and completes assignment book daily	•		•	•
Breaks down tasks and completes on time				•

Topics to revisit in our next meeting...

A Note from Author Lisa Dieker

How are you gathering data on IEP progress? I believe students with disabilities should be given credit for the two curriculua (the general education curriculum and their IEPs) they are expected to master. Too many times students are only evaluated on the general education curriculum. Yet they are not successful in the general education curriculum because of what's on their IEPs. Therefore, be certain you are teaching to both and evaluating both areas.

Professional Development Resources

Harbort, G., Gunter, P.L., Hull, K., Brown, Q., Venn, M.L., Wiley, L.P., & Wiley, E.W. (2007). Behaviors of teachers in co-taught classes in a secondary school. *Teacher Education and Special Education*, 30(1), 13-23.

Dieker, L. A., Finnegan, L., Grillo, K. & Garland, D. (2013). Special education in the science classroom: A co-teaching scenario *Science Scope*, 37(4), 18-22.

Engineering for K-12
http://www.egfi-k12.org/

Minute Physics
https://www.youtube.com/user/minutephysics?feature=watch

Follow-up To-Do List
Educator 1

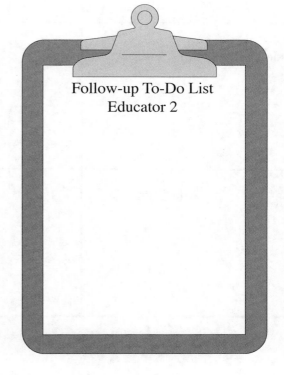

Follow-up To-Do List
Educator 2

Week of _____

Subject _____

Class Hour _____

Target Students
_____
_____
_____
_____
_____

Does your overall lesson meet the needs of students who cannot ...

Day/Date	Big Idea/Goals	Lesson Activities	Assessment	
			Standard	Adapted/Modified
Monday	All / Some			
Tuesday	All / Some			
Wednesday	All / Some			
Thursday	All / Some			
Friday	All / Some			

This page is designed to be completed by Educator On

Co-Teaching Structures:

(O) one lead, one support
(S) station teaching
(P) parallel teaching
(A) alternative teaching
(T) team teaching

Students with Special Needs

_____
_____
_____
_____
_____
_____

☐ Walk ☐ Talk ☐ See ☐ Hear ☐ Behave or ☐ Learn the way you traditionally teach?

Co-Teaching Structure	Academic Adaptations (as needed for gifted students and students with disabilities)	Behavioral Adaptations	Materials/ Support Needed	Performance Data and Notes

This page is designed to be completed by Educator Two.

Week of _____

Subject _____

Class Hour _____

Target Students
_____
_____
_____
_____
_____

Does your overall lesson meet the needs of students who cannot ...

Day/Date	Big Idea/Goals	Lesson Activities	Assessment	
			Standard	Adapted/Modified
Monday	All / Some			
Tuesday	All / Some			
Wednesday	All / Some			
Thursday	All / Some			
Friday	All / Some			

This page is designed to be completed by Educator On

Co-Teaching Structures:
- (O) one lead, one support
- (S) station teaching
- (P) parallel teaching
- (A) alternative teaching
- (T) team teaching

Students with Special Needs

_____
_____
_____
_____
_____
_____

□ Walk □ Talk □ See □ Hear □ Behave or □ Learn the way you traditionally teach?

Co-Teaching Structure	Academic Adaptations (as needed for gifted students and students with disabilities)	Behavioral Adaptations	Materials/ Support Needed	Performance Data and Notes

This page is designed to be completed by Educator Two.

Week of _____

Subject _____

Class Hour _____

Target Students

_____
_____
_____
_____
_____

Does your overall lesson meet the needs of students who cannot ...

Day/Date	Big Idea/Goals	Lesson Activities	Assessment	
			Standard	Adapted/Modified
Monday	All / Some			
Tuesday	All / Some			
Wednesday	All / Some			
Thursday	All / Some			
Friday	All / Some			

This page is designed to be completed by Educator Only

Co-Teaching Structures:

(O) one lead, one support
(S) station teaching
(P) parallel teaching
(A) alternative teaching
(T) team teaching

Strategy Suggestion...
Turned paper – Turn notebook paper sideways to use lines for math problems. Provide answers or fill-in-the-blank questions.

Students with Special Needs

_____

_____

_____

_____

_____

☐ Walk ☐ Talk ☐ See ☐ Hear ☐ Behave or ☐ Learn the way you traditionally teach?

Co-Teaching Structure	Academic Adaptations (as needed for gifted students and students with disabilities)	Behavioral Adaptations	Materials/ Support Needed	Performance Data and Notes

This page is designed to be completed by Educator Two.

-77-

Week of _____

Subject _____

Class Hour _____

Target Students
_____
_____
_____
_____
_____

Does your overall lesson meet the needs of students who cannot ...

Day/Date	Big Idea/Goals	Lesson Activities	Assessment	
			Standard	Adapted/Modified
Monday	All / Some			
Tuesday	All / Some			
Wednesday	All / Some			
Thursday	All / Some			
Friday	All / Some			

This page is designed to be completed by Educator On

Co-Teaching Structures:

(O) one lead, one support
(S) station teaching
(P) parallel teaching
(A) alternative teaching
(T) team teaching

Strategy Suggestion...
Expectations: State your academic and behavioral expectations at the beginning of each class.

Students with Special Needs
_____
_____
_____
_____
_____

☐ Walk ☐ Talk ☐ See ☐ Hear ☐ Behave or ☐ Learn the way you traditionally teach?

Co-Teaching Structure	Academic Adaptations (as needed for gifted students and students with disabilities)	Behavioral Adaptations	Materials/ Support Needed	Performance Data and Notes

This page is designed to be completed by Educator Two.

Week 28 Co-Teaching Progress Check-up

Meeting Agenda
Suggested time: 30 minutes

Now is a good time to schedule a meeting between co-teaching partners to reflect on the experience to-date. Use the following agenda to guide the discussion.

1. Discuss each of the questions in the Reflective Framework (below).

2. Read and discuss the Author's Note (next page).

3. Record your thoughts and notes in the space provided for
    - Ideas
    - Topics to revisit in our next meeting
    - Follow-up to-do list for each team member

Reflective Framework

Colleague Janet Hill has given me permission to summarize some of her key ideas for supporting students before/during/after testing. Try them out with your students!

Before the Test
- Create and use concept maps, study guides, and graphic organizers
- Prepare note cards
- Determine test modifications
- Take practice tests
- Hold individual and group review sessions
- Practice test taking strategies

During the Test
- Check everyone's anxiety level
- Give immediate feedback
- Complete one problem/question in every section
- Request teacher assistance as needed
- Complete test at alternate site if necessary
- Practice self monitoring
- Utilize extended time (if provided)

After the Test
- Retake all or part of the test (if permittable)
- Make corrections on incorrect problems
- Consider alternative grading approaches such as partial credit, grade only a subset of questions, etc.

Topics to revisit in our next meeting...

A Note from Author Lisa Dieker

Brain research informs us that learning and memory is greatly impacted by anxiety. This month I have provided you with some tips from a colleague to assist with testing.

Keep in mind that a discussion related to state proficiency testing should be a core part of the planning and the accommodations discussed for students with disabilities. Remember, students must be taught how to use their accommodations prior to state testing so make teaching these skills part of your planning.

Professional Development Resources

McDuffie, K.,Mastropieri, M.A.., & Scruggs, T.E. (2009). Promoting success in content area classes: Is value added through co-teaching? *Exceptional Children*, 75, 493-510.

Pearl, C., Dieker, L. A., & Kirkpatrick, R. (2012). A five year retrospective on the Arkansas department of education co-teaching project. *Journal of Staff Development*, 38(4), 571-587.

Newsmap
http://newsmap.jp/

Parent Center Hub on Co-teaching
http://www.parentcenterhub.org/repository/coteaching/

Follow-up To-Do List
Educator 1

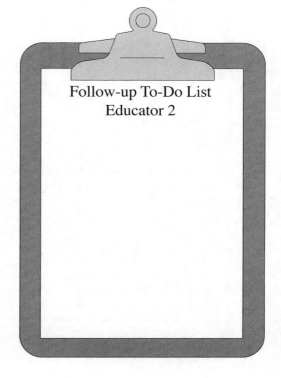

Follow-up To-Do List
Educator 2

Week of _____

Subject _____

Class Hour _____

Strategy Suggestion...
RIDGES – a problem solving strategy:
R – Read the problem carefully
I – I know __ from the problem
D – Draw a picture
G – Goal statement from the problem
E – Equation development to set up the computation
S – Solve the equation

Target Students

_____
_____
_____
_____
_____

Does your overall lesson meet the needs of students who cannot ...

Day/Date	Big Idea/Goals	Lesson Activities	Assessment	
			Standard	Adapted/Modified
Monday	All / Some			
Tuesday	All / Some			
Wednesday	All / Some			
Thursday	All / Some			
Friday	All / Some			

This page is designed to be completed by Educator On

o-Teaching Structures:

(O) one lead, one support
(S) station teaching
(P) parallel teaching
(A) alternative teaching
(T) team teaching

Strategy Suggestion...

SLOBS – a math borrowing strategy:
  S – Smaller, follow steps;
  L – Larger; leap to substract;
  O – Cross Off number in next column;
  B – Borrow by taking one 10 and adding to the
      next column;
  S – Subtract

Students with Special Needs
_____
_____
_____
_____
_____

☐ Walk ☐ Talk ☐ See ☐ Hear ☐ Behave or ☐ Learn the way you traditionally teach?

o-Teaching tructure	Academic Adaptations (as needed for gifted students and students with disabilities)	Behavioral Adaptations	Materials/ Support Needed	Performance Data and Notes

his page is designed to be completed by Educator Two.

Week of _____

Subject _____

Class Hour _____

Strategy Suggestion...
Error analysis – Teach students to use error-pattern analysis to identify their areas of incorrect logic.

Target Students
_____
_____
_____
_____
_____

Does your overall lesson meet the needs of students who cannot ...

Day/Date	Big Idea/Goals	Lesson Activities	Assessment	
			Standard	Adapted/Modified
Monday	All / Some			
Tuesday	All / Some			
Wednesday	All / Some			
Thursday	All / Some			
Friday	All / Some			

This page is designed to be completed by Educator On

Co-Teaching Structures:
- (O) one lead, one support
- (S) station teaching
- (P) parallel teaching
- (A) alternative teaching
- (T) team teaching

Strategy Suggestion...
Individualized homework – Give students opportunities to develop their own homework after offering examples.

Students with Special Needs
_____
_____
_____
_____
_____

☐ Walk ☐ Talk ☐ See ☐ Hear ☐ Behave or ☐ Learn the way you traditionally teach?

Co-Teaching Structure	Academic Adaptations (as needed for gifted students and students with disabilities)	Behavioral Adaptations	Materials/ Support Needed	Performance Data and Notes

This page is designed to be completed by Educator Two.

-85-

Week of _____

Subject _____

Class Hour _____

Target Students
_____
_____
_____
_____
_____

Does your overall lesson meet the needs of students who cannot ...

Day/Date	Big Idea/Goals	Lesson Activities	Assessment	
			Standard	Adapted/Modified
Monday	All / Some			
Tuesday	All / Some			
Wednesday	All / Some			
Thursday	All / Some			
Friday	All / Some			

This page is designed to be completed by Educator On

Co-Teaching Structures:

(O) one lead, one support

(S) station teaching

(P) parallel teaching

(A) alternative teaching

(T) team teaching

Strategy Suggestion...
Assure student access – Ask your occupational or physical therapist to review the accessibility of your lab space and instructional materials.

Students with Special Needs

_____

_____

_____

_____

_____

☐ Walk ☐ Talk ☐ See ☐ Hear ☐ Behave or ☐ Learn the way you traditionally teach?

Co-Teaching Structure	Academic Adaptations (as needed for gifted students and students with disabilities)	Behavioral Adaptations	Materials/ Support Needed	Performance Data and Notes

This page is designed to be completed by Educator Two.

Week of _____

Subject _____

Class Hour _____

Target Students
_____
_____
_____
_____
_____

Does your overall lesson meet the needs of students who cannot ...

Day/Date	Big Idea/Goals	Lesson Activities	Assessment	
			Standard	Adapted/Modified
Monday	All / Some			
Tuesday	All / Some			
Wednesday	All / Some			
Thursday	All / Some			
Friday	All / Some			

This page is designed to be completed by Educator On

Co-Teaching Structures:
(O) one lead, one support
(S) station teaching
(P) parallel teaching
(A) alternative teaching
(T) team teaching

Strategy Suggestion...
Alternative lessons outcomes –
Allow students to demonstrate under-
standing of a concept at a different
level or in a different format.

Students with Special Needs
_____
_____
_____
_____
_____

☐ Walk ☐ Talk ☐ See ☐ Hear ☐ Behave or ☐ Learn the way you traditionally teach?

Co-Teaching Structure	Academic Adaptations (as needed for gifted students and students with disabilities)	Behavioral Adaptations	Materials/ Support Needed	Performance Data and Notes

This page is designed to be completed by Educator Two.

Week 32 Co-Teaching Progress Check-up

Meeting Agenda
Suggested time: 30 minutes

Now is a good time to schedule a meeting between co-teaching partners to reflect on the experience to-date. Use the following agenda to guide the discussion.

1. Discuss each of the questions in the Reflective Framework (below).

2. Read and discuss the Author's Note (next page).

3. Record your thoughts and notes in the space provided for
   - Ideas
   - Topics to revisit in our next meeting
   - Follow-up to-do list for each team member

Reflective Framework

As the end of the year approaches, now is a good time to do a mental health check-up. Discuss the following questions:

• Are you ending the year with a list of 10 positive things you accomplished?

• Can you list 5 or more reasons as to why you should co-teach again next year?

• Have you shared with administrators how you would like your co-teaching schedule to be structured for next year?

• What 1-2 things will you focus on improving in your co-teaching relationship(s) next year?

• What is the nicest thing you will do for yourselves over the summer?

• Have you ordered a new co-teaching plan book for next year?

Topics to revisit in our next meeting...

A Note from Author Lisa Dieker

The last few weeks of the school year always present mixed feelings of anticipation for summer and a need to be sure all students are ready for the next grade level. In the weeks remaining, how can you strategically plan to ensure they are ready?

To help put a positive spin on the daily chore of teaching, go out of your way to affirm all your colleagues, and especially your co-teaching peer. If you are tired, you should be! Research shows as a teacher you make over 1,300 decisions a day. Use these decisions wisely and stay positive!

Professional Development Resources

Damore, S. J., & Murray, C. (2009). Urban elementary school teachers' perspectives regarding collaborative teaching practices. *Remedial and Special Education*, 30(4), 234-244.

Murawski, W. W., & Hughes, C. E. (2009). Response to Intervention, collaboration, and co-teaching: A necessary combination for successful systemic change. *Preventing School Failure*, 53(4), 67-77.

Free Rice (vocabulary)
http://freerice.com/

Voki (create an avatar)
http://voki.com/

Follow-up To-Do List
Educator 1

Follow-up To-Do List
Educator 2

Week of _____

Subject _____

Class Hour _____

Strategy Suggestion...
Use different modes of learning – Good teaching involves all the senses (seeing, touching, tasting, hearing, and smelling). How can you provide instruction in multiple modalities?

Target Students

_____
_____
_____
_____
_____

Does your overall lesson meet the needs of students who cannot ...

Day/Date	Big Idea/Goals	Lesson Activities	Assessment	
			Standard	Adapted/Modified
Monday	All / Some			
Tuesday	All / Some			
Wednesday	All / Some			
Thursday	All / Some			
Friday	All / Some			

Co-Teaching Structures:

(O) one lead, one support

(S) station teaching

(P) parallel teaching

(A) alternative teaching

(T) team teaching

Students with Special Needs

_____
_____
_____
_____
_____

☐ Walk ☐ Talk ☐ See ☐ Hear ☐ Behave or ☐ Learn the way you traditionally teach?

Co-Teaching Structure	Academic Adaptations (as needed for gifted students and students with disabilities)	Behavioral Adaptations	Materials/ Support Needed	Performance Data and Notes

This page is designed to be completed by Educator Two.

Week of _____
Subject _____
Class Hour _____

Strategy Suggestion...
Assigning homework – Ask students to review their homework and mark what they believe is doable and "not doable." Talk it over individually. Modify the assignment as appropriate.

Target Students
_____
_____
_____
_____
_____

Does your overall lesson meet the needs of students who cannot ...

Day/Date	Big Idea/Goals	Lesson Activities	Assessment	
			Standard	Adapted/Modified
Monday	All / Some			
Tuesday	All / Some			
Wednesday	All / Some			
Thursday	All / Some			
Friday	All / Some			

This page is designed to be completed by Educator On

Co-Teaching Structures:

(O) one lead, one support
(S) station teaching
(P) parallel teaching
(A) alternative teaching
(T) team teaching

Students with Special Needs

_____
_____
_____
_____
_____
_____

☐ Walk ☐ Talk ☐ See ☐ Hear ☐ Behave or ☐ Learn the way you traditionally teach?

Co-Teaching Structure	Academic Adaptations (as needed for gifted students and students with disabilities)	Behavioral Adaptations	Materials/ Support Needed	Performance Data and Notes

This page is designed to be completed by Educator Two.

Week of _____

Subject _____

Class Hour _____

Target Students
_____
_____
_____
_____
_____

Does your overall lesson meet the needs of students who cannot ...

Day/Date	Big Idea/Goals	Lesson Activities	Assessment	
			Standard	Adapted/Modified
Monday	All / Some			
Tuesday	All / Some			
Wednesday	All / Some			
Thursday	All / Some			
Friday	All / Some			

This page is designed to be completed by Educator On

o-Teaching Structures:
- (O) one lead, one support
- (S) station teaching
- (P) parallel teaching
- (A) alternative teaching
- (T) team teaching

Strategy Suggestion...
Create a checklist – Make a list of the major skills for each quarter and ask the student or a special educator to help assess what skills a student can or cannot easily accomplish.

Students with Special Needs

_____
_____
_____
_____
_____

☐ Walk ☐ Talk ☐ See ☐ Hear ☐ Behave or ☐ Learn the way you traditionally teach?

o-Teaching tructure	Academic Adaptations (as needed for gifted students and students with disabilities)	Behavioral Adaptations	Materials/ Support Needed	Performance Data and Notes

This page is designed to be completed by Educator Two.

Week of _____

Subject _____

Class Hour _____

Strategy Suggestion...
Coordinate your material with content area material – Consider how you can reinforce all the subject areas that students experience each day (e.g., use words from P.E. in your writing assignments). All students will learn more effectively when subject areas are connected.

Target Students
_____
_____
_____
_____
_____

Does your overall lesson meet the needs of students who cannot ...

Day/Date	Big Idea/Goals	Lesson Activities	Assessment	
			Standard	Adapted/Modified
Monday	All / Some			
Tuesday	All / Some			
Wednesday	All / Some			
Thursday	All / Some			
Friday	All / Some			

This page is designed to be completed by Educator On

Co-Teaching Structures:

- (O) one lead, one support
- (S) station teaching
- (P) parallel teaching
- (A) alternative teaching
- (T) team teaching

Students with Special Needs

_____
_____
_____
_____
_____

☐ Walk ☐ Talk ☐ See ☐ Hear ☐ Behave or ☐ Learn the way you traditionally teach?

Co-Teaching Structure	Academic Adaptations (as needed for gifted students and students with disabilities)	Behavioral Adaptations	Materials/ Support Needed	Performance Data and Notes

This page is designed to be completed by Educator Two.

Week 36 Co-Teaching Progress Check-up

Meeting Agenda
Suggested time: 30 minutes

Now is a good time to schedule a meeting between co-teaching partners to reflect on the experience to-date. Use the following agenda to guide the discussion.

1. Discuss each of the questions in the Reflective Framework (below).

2. Read and discuss the Author's Note (next page).

3. Record your thoughts and notes in the space provided for
   - Ideas
   - Topics to revisit in our next meeting
   - Follow-up to-do list for each team member

Reflective Framework

As the school year draws to a close, now would be a good time to carefully consider the success individual students have achieved this past year. Use the following discussion questions to guide the conversation:

- How do you both feel about your roles as co-teachers?

- Are there changes you need to make before the start of next year?

- Are there other support staff you need to have involved in ensuring the success of all students (e.g., administrator, social worker, guidance counselor)?

- Have you clearly discussed the curricular expectations for the next year as well as the IEP needs of students in the class?

- Will there be state or proficiency testing that will occur next fall? If so, how have you prepared the students and will there be modifications made for the students with disabilities?

- Have you both shared something positive about your co-teaching relationship with each other, a colleague, and an administrator?

- What are the best things you plan to do over the summer break?